CCSS **Genre** Expository Text

Essential Question
How are offspring like their parents?

Animal Families

by Deborah November

Chapter 1

Deer Families

People take care of their babies when they are small. Animals take care of their babies, too. Some animals even live in families.

Baby Deer

A deer is a mammal just like you. Mammals are not hatched from eggs. Deer mothers have one to three babies at a time. The babies, or **fawns**, walk soon after birth. They're a little shaky, but they can walk!

Deer mothers feed their babies for about two months.

2

Deer eat fruits, nuts, and leaves.

Fawns have no smell. This way, their **enemies** cannot find them. The mother deer hides her fawns in bushes. Fawns also have spots. That helps them hide in the leaves. The spots go away when the deer grow older.

Young Deer

Young deer stay with their mothers for a year or two. After that, they can take care of themselves. **Bucks**, or male deer, begin to grow antlers. The antlers take a few months to start growing.

Female deer, called does, do not grow antlers.

Antlers are made from bone.

Antlers break off once a year. Then they grow back. As the deer becomes an adult, he usually has bigger antlers. The antlers have more points on them if the deer is healthy.

Chapter 2

Babies in Pouches

Some animals have a **pouch**. The mother carries her babies inside.

Kangaroos

A baby kangaroo, or **joey,** is about the size of a grape at birth. It grows very big. The giant red kangaroo is the biggest Australian kangaroo.

Most kangaroos live in Australia.

Tier Und Naturfotografie J & C Sohns/Stockimage/Getty Images

Kangaroos are a special kind of mammal.

A mother kangaroo may take care of three babies at the same time! One is inside her. One is in her pouch. The other one is out of her pouch. She still gives it milk.

The kangaroo comes out of the pouch. It begins to hop! Kangaroos cannot walk the way that humans can. Their strong legs are built for hopping.

Kangaroos hop on their back feet.

Koalas sleep most of the day.

Koalas

Koalas live in their mothers' pouches too. They stay in the pouch for five to seven months. The mother koala and her offspring, or baby, do not look like each other at first. When a koala is born, it is tiny and hairless. When a koala grows up, it is covered with thick, gray fur. Koalas have special paws. They use these paws to groom, or clean themselves.

Chapter 3

Animals from Eggs

Some animals lay eggs with babies inside. The parents care for the eggs.

Penguins

Baby penguins, or chicks, hatch from eggs. The mother lays her egg and goes to find food. The father watches over the egg for about 65 days. He keeps it warm near his feet.

Penguins are birds, but they cannot fly.

Jochem D Wiinands/Photographer's Choice/Getty Images

Penguins know when their baby is calling them.

The father penguin has nothing to eat all that time. Can you imagine? When the baby penguin hatches, or comes out of the egg, the mother comes back. Then it is the father's turn to go and eat. The baby penguin is covered with gray feathers. When the penguin grows up, it will look just like its parents.

Alligators

Alligator mothers lay at least 20 eggs. The mother watches over the eggs in the **nest**. Then the eggs hatch. The mother hears noises from the babies. That is how she knows they are ready to come out of the nest.

Many alligators live in Florida.

George Shelley/CORBIS

Alligators are good swimmers.

The babies are very small. They are only about six inches long. The alligator may look scary. But she is a very good mother. She protects her babies. She helps them stay alive.

Alligator mothers take care of their babies for about two years. The babies can grow as much as one foot every year. Just think how big you would be if you were an alligator!

Animal mothers and fathers take good care of their babies. Animal families are like human families in many ways.

Alligators, like lizards and snakes, are reptiles.

Jonathan Blair/CORBIS

Respond to Reading

Summarize

Use important details to summarize *Animal Families*.

Main Topic		
Detail	Detail	Detail

Text Evidence

1. How do you know that *Animal Families* is expository text? Genre

2. Compare and contrast how different animals care for their babies. Main Topic and Key Details

3. What word on page 4 also means "to see something"? Multiple-Meaning Words

4. Write about how father penguins take care of eggs. Write About Reading

Compare Texts

Read about baby tadpoles and how they become frogs.

Tadpoles into Frogs

When tadpoles, or baby frogs, are born, they do not look like frogs. Frogs begin as eggs. The eggs are under the water.

When the egg hatches, the tadpole is born.

Baby tadpoles look like fish.

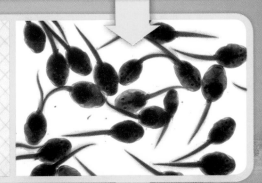

Tadpoles have a tail, a mouth, and gills. They use the gills to breathe.

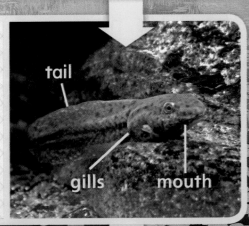

tail

gills

mouth

Then the tadpole begins to grow legs.

The tadpole's tail disappears.

Now the tadpole is a frog! He hops out of the water onto the land.

Make Connections

How do tadpoles grow to be like their parents? **Essential Question**

How are other baby animals like their parents? **Text to Text**

Glossary

bucks *(BUKS)* male deer *(page 4)*

fawns *(FAWNZ)* baby deer *(page 2)*

enemies *(EN-uh-meez)* those that may want to hurt someone *(page 3)*

joey *(JOH-ee)* a baby kangaroo *(page 6)*

nest *(NEST)* a place where animals lay eggs or raise their babies *(page 12)*

pouch *(POWCH)* a pocket on some female animals used to carry babies *(page 6)*

Index

Focus on
Science

Purpose To find out how baby animals are like their parents

What to Do

Step 1 With a partner, choose two animals from this book.

Step 2 Draw a picture of each animal as a baby.

Step 3 Switch pages with your partner. Draw each animal as an adult.

Conclusion Talk about how the baby is like the adult. Then talk about how it is different. How does the animal change as it grows?